NATIONAL GEOGRAPHIC

STUDENT'S BOOK STARTER

Joan Kang Shin

AUTHOR
Diane Pinkley

Unit 0 . . . . **2**

Unit 1 My School **6**

Unit 2 My Toys **14**

Unit 3 My Family **22**

Unit 4 My Body **30**

Units 1–4 Review **38**

Unit 5 Stories **40**

Unit 6 I Like Food **48**

Unit 7 Clothes **56**

Unit 8 Animals **64**

Units 5–8 Review **72**

Writing **74**

Cutouts **83**

Stickers

NATIONAL GEOGRAPHIC
L E A R N I N G

Australia · Brazil · Mexico · Singapore · United Kingdom · United States

1 Look and listen. Say. TR:A2

Sit down.

Stand up.

Open your book.

Close your book.

3 **Look and listen.** Say. TR: A4

a book　　　**a red book**　　　**a blue book**

4 **Point and say.**

5 **Look and listen.** Say. Trace. TR: A5

 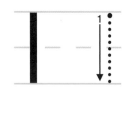  

6 **Look and listen.** Stick and say. TR: A6

1	2
3	4

7 **Listen and say.** TR: A7

hello

goodbye

8 **Listen.** Which words have the sound? Tick. ✔ TR: A8

sound	word I	word 2	word 3
I			
2			

9 **Listen and chant.** TR: A9

Hello, hello.

Hi there, hi.

Time to go.

Bye, goodbye!

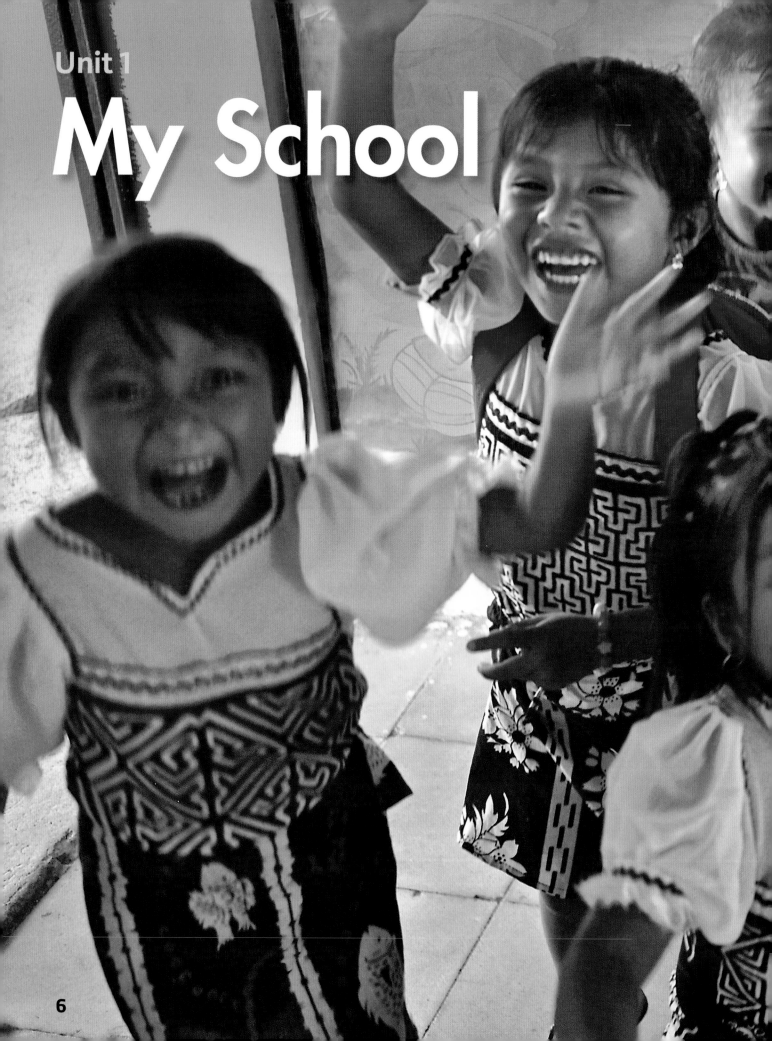

My School

Students in Ustupu Island, Panama

1 **Listen and point.** TR: A10

2 **Point and say.**

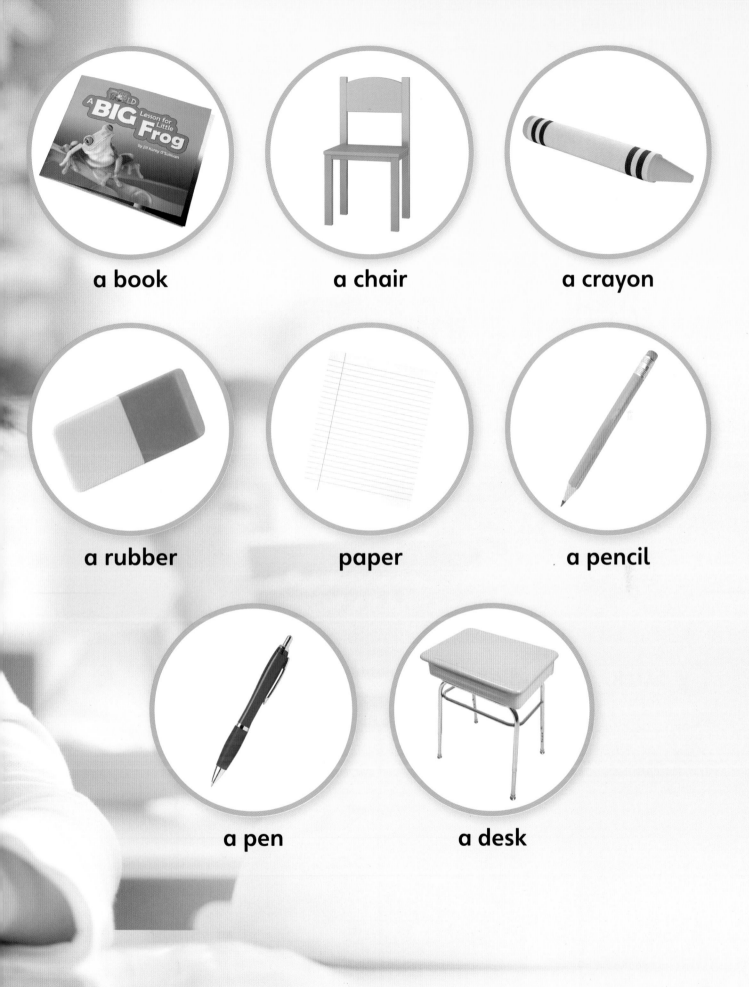

a book

a chair

a crayon

a rubber

paper

a pencil

a pen

a desk

3 Listen and (circle.) TR: A11

1.

2.

3.

4.

4 Listen and say. Talk. TR: A12

What is it?

It's a chair.

5 Stick. Ask and answer.

1	2	3	4
5	6	7	8

6 **Listen and point.** Say. TR: A13

green   yellow

7 **Listen and colour.** TR: A14

8 **Listen.** Count and say. Trace. TR: A15

9 **Listen.** Count and say. TR: A16

10 **Listen and say.** Cut out the cards on page 83. Listen. Put the cards in the boxes. Say. TR: A17

11 **Listen and say.** TR: A18

12 **Listen.** Which words have the sound? Tick. ✔ TR: A19

sound	word 1	word 2	word 3
1			
2			
3			

13 **Listen and chant.** TR: A20

I've got some paper.

I've got a pen.

I've got a pencil.

Let's draw again!

14 Listen to the story. TR: A21

Time for School

Time for school! Sit down, please.

Four crayons for you.

A green pen for Robot. Two yellow pencils for you, Teddy.

OK. Let's draw!

15 Do you like the story? Circle.

Unit 2
My Toys

1 Listen and point. TR: A23

2 Point and say.

a ball

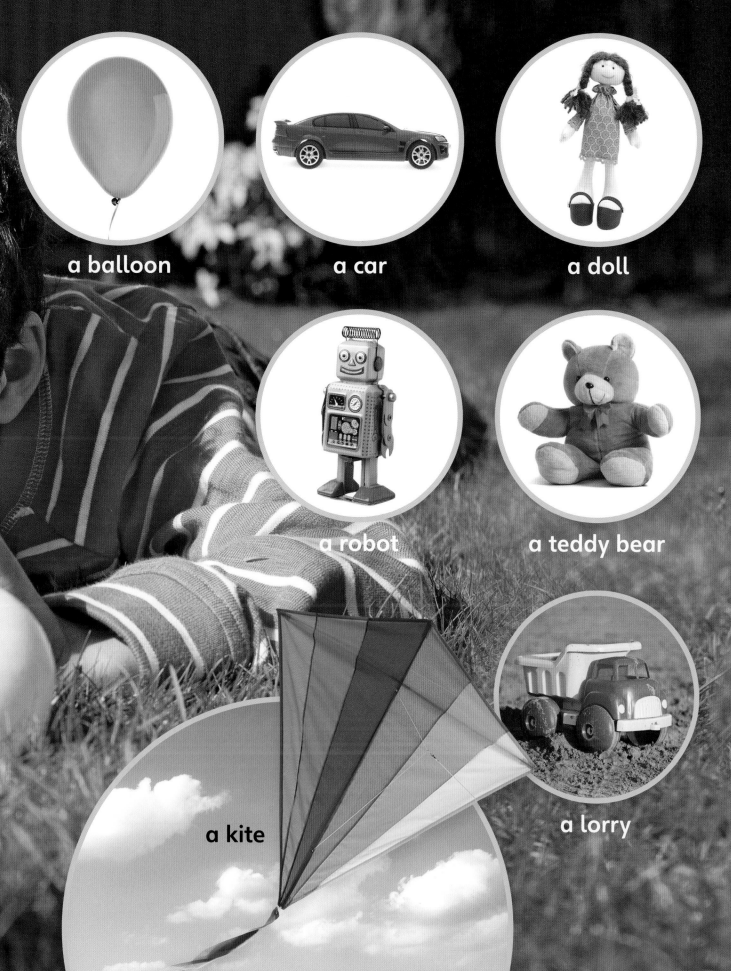

a balloon

a car

a doll

a robot

a teddy bear

a kite

a lorry

17

1.

2.

3.

4.

4 **Listen and say.** Talk. TR: A25

Is it a doll?

No, it isn't.

Is it a teddy bear?

Yes, it is.

5 **Listen.** Stick. TR: A26

1	2	3	4
5	6	7	8

6 **Listen and point.** Say. TR: A27

brown   orange

7 **Listen and colour.** TR: A28

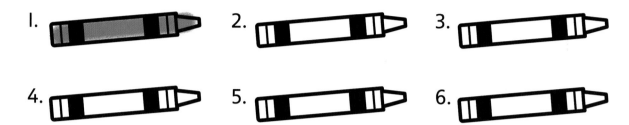

1.   2.   3.

4.   5.   6.

8 **Listen.** Count and say. Trace. TR: A29

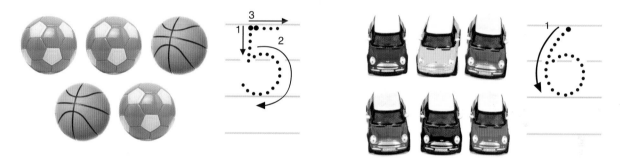

9 **Listen.** Count and say. TR: A30

10 **Listen and say.** Cut out the cards on page 85. Play the game. TR: A31

Four balls.

Five kites. Your turn!

19

11 **Listen and say.** TR: A32

12 **Listen.** Which words have the sound? Tick. ✔ TR: A33

sound	word 1	word 2	word 3
1			
2			
3			

13 **Listen and chant.** TR: A34

Dolls and robots
and more toys.
Balls and kites
for girls and boys!

14 **Listen to the story.** TR: A35

Birthday Boy

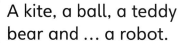

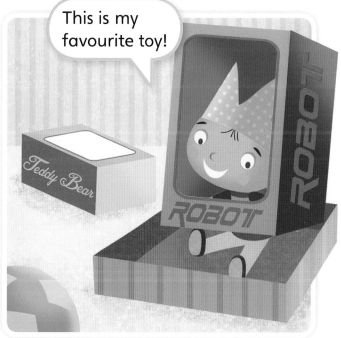

15 **Do you like the story?** Circle.

My Family

Mother and children on a train, Vietnam

2 **Point and say.**

grandma

grandpa

me

sister

father

mother

brother

a kitchen

a bathroom

a bedroom

a living room

3 **Listen and** (**circle.**) TR: A38

4 **Listen and say.** Talk. TR: A39

Who's this?

It's my brother.

5 **Listen.** Look at the rooms. Stick and say. TR: A40

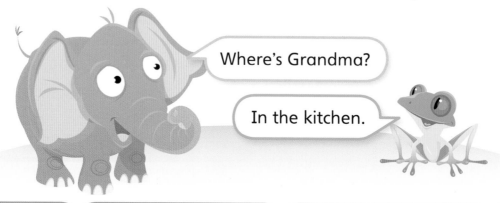

Where's Grandma?

In the kitchen.

6 **Listen and point.** Say. TR: A41

black   white

7 **Listen and colour.** TR: A42

1.   2.   3.

4.   5.   6.

8 **Listen.** Count and say. Trace. TR: A43

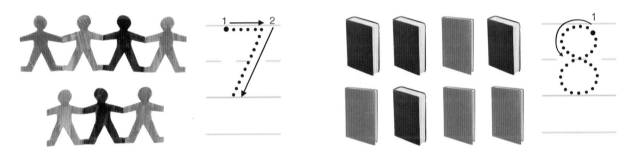

9 **Listen.** Count and say. TR: A44

10 **Listen and say.** Cut out five cards on page 87. Ask and answer. TR: A45

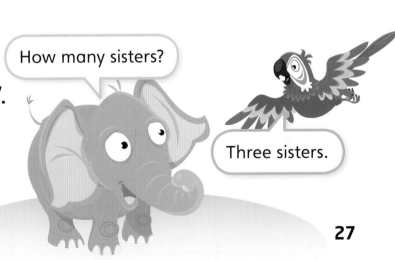

How many sisters?

Three sisters.

27

11 Listen and say. TR: A46

12 Listen. Which words have the sound? Tick. ✔ TR: A47

sound	word 1	word 2	word 3
1			
2			
3			

13 Listen and chant. TR: A48

I love my grandpa!

Oh yes, I do.

My brothers and

my sisters love him, too.

14 Listen to the story. TR: A49

Eight is Great

Look! My family is big!

One, two, three, four ...

... five, six, seven, eight brothers and sisters!

And eight cats, eight dogs, eight birds and eight fish!

15 Do you like the story? Circle.

29

My Body

Wodaabe men, Niger

1 **Listen and point.** TR: A51

2 **Point and say.**

ears

hair

eyes

a nose

a mouth

32

arms

hands

legs

feet

3 **Listen.** Draw lines. TR: A52

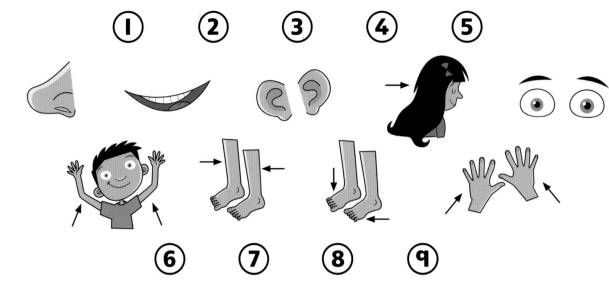

4 **Listen and say.** TR: A53

I've got two hands.

She's got two hands.

5 **Listen.** Stick and say. TR: A54

6 **Listen and point.** What is missing? Say. TR: A55

1	2	3	4
5	6	7	8

7 **Listen and point.** Say. TR: A56

pink purple

8 **Listen and colour.** TR: A57

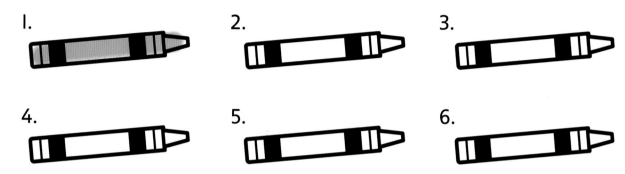

1.   2.   3.

4.   5.   6.

9 **Listen.** Count and say. Trace. TR:A58

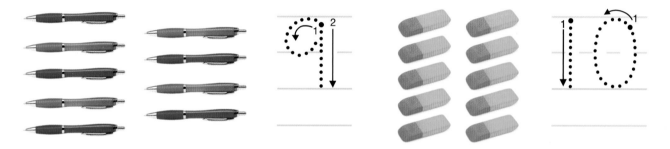

10 **Cut out the cards on page 89.** Listen.
Put the cards in order. Say. TR: A59

11 **Use the rest of the cards on page 89.**
Put the cards in order. Say.

Two orange kites.

OK. Three blue books.

12 **Listen and say.** TR: A60

13 **Listen.** Which words have the sound? Tick. ✔ TR: A61

sound	word 1	word 2	word 3
1			
2			
3			

14 **Listen and chant.** TR: A62

One mouth for me,
Two arms for you.
Two eyes for me,
Two legs for you!

It's Me!

Mum's in the kitchen.

The robot's in the kitchen, too.

Oh, no! A robot with four ears and three eyes!

Don't worry, Mum. It's me!

16 **Do you like the story?** Circle.

Review

Start

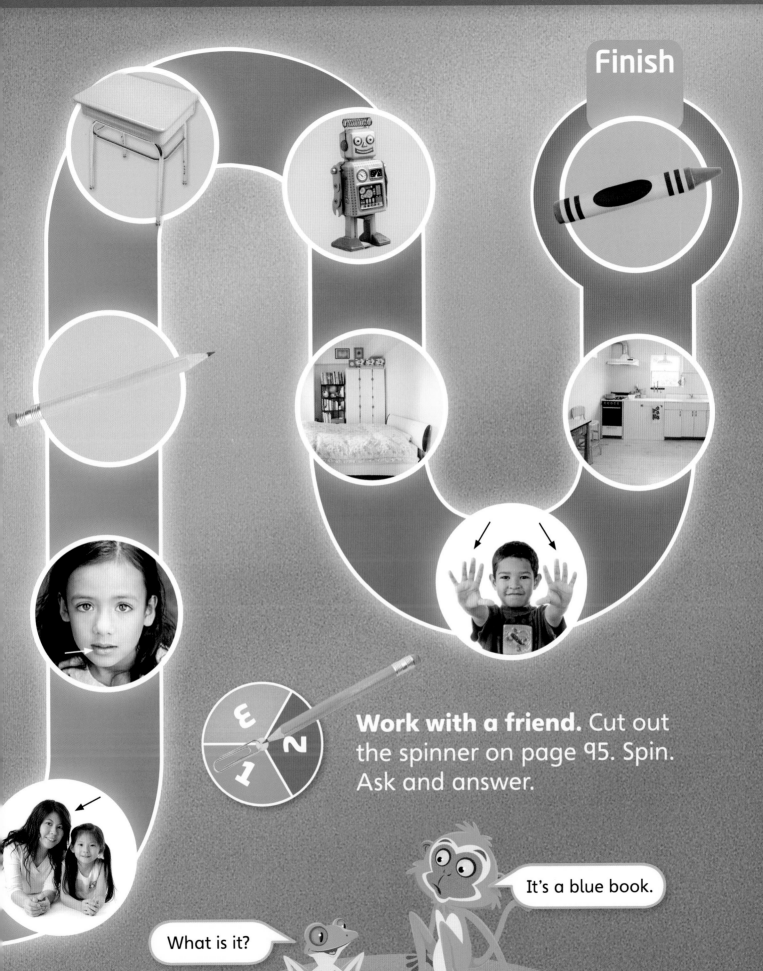

Finish

Work with a friend. Cut out the spinner on page 95. Spin. Ask and answer.

It's a blue book.

What is it?

39

Stories

Neuschwanstein Castle, Bavaria, Germany

2 **Point and say.**

a crown

happy

sad

a queen

a princess

a king

a frog

a friend

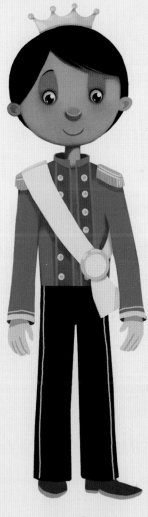

a prince

3 **Listen and (circle) yes or no.** TR:B3

1.  yes   no

2. yes   no

3. yes   no

4.  yes   no

5. yes   no

6. yes   no

7. yes   no

8.  yes   no

4 **Listen and say.** TR: B4

I want a friend.

I want a crown, please.

5 **Listen.** Stick and say. TR: B5

1	2	3	4

6 Listen and point. Say. TR: B6

gold   silver

7 Listen and stick. TR: B7

1	2	3	4

8 Listen. Count and say. TR: B8

9 Cut out the game board and the cards on page 91.
Listen. Put the cards into two groups. Say. TR: B9

10 **Listen and say.** TR: B10

11 **Listen.** Which words have the sound? Tick. ✔ TR: B11

sound	word 1	word 2	word 3
1			
2			
3			

12 **Listen and chant.** TR: B12

The prince wants silver.
The queen wants gold.
The king wants a crown
of silver and gold!

46

New Friends

You, snake! Stop! Go away!

Thank you! Now you're a prince with a gold crown!

I'm sad. I want a friend.

We're your friends. A prince, a princess and a frog!

14 **Do you like the story?** Circle.

Unit 6
I Like Food

Brothers eating noodles
in Shigatse, Tibet

49

1 **Listen and point.** TR: B15

2 **Point and say.**

bananas

bread

milk

biscuits

water

orange juice

rice

chicken

noodles

51

3 Listen and (circle.) TR: B16

4 Listen and say. Talk. TR: B17

I like noodles.

I don't like noodles.

5 Stick. Talk.

6 **Listen and point.** Say. TR: B18

a circle   a square

7 **Listen and colour.** TR: B19

1. ⬤ ☐   4. ◯ ☐

2. ◯ ☐   5. ◯ ☐

3. ◯ ☐   6. ◯ ☐

8 **Listen.** Count and say. TR: B20

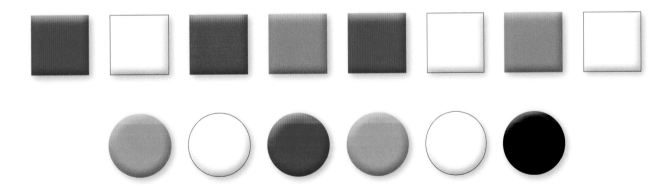

9 **Cut out the cards on page 93.** Listen.
Put the cards in order. Say. TR: B21

10 Listen and say. TR: B22

11 Listen. Which words have the sound? Tick. ✔ TR: B23

sound	word 1	word 2	word 3
1			
2			
3			

12 Listen and chant. TR: B24

I like chicken.
I like rice.
I like noodles.
They're so nice!

13 Listen to the story. TR: B25

A Picnic

It's lunchtime. Look! A picnic!

I like apples.

I don't like apples.
I like bananas.

I like bread.

I don't like bread.
I like biscuits.

Yum yum! Let's eat!

14 Do you like the story? (Circle.)

Unit 7
Clothes

A dancer in Mexico

1 **Listen and point.** TR: B27

2 **Point and say.**

a coat

58

a hat

a dress

trousers

a T-shirt

shoes

shorts

a skirt

socks

3 **Listen.** Draw lines. TR: B28

① ② ③ ④ ⑤

⑥ ⑦ ⑧ ⑨

4 **Listen and say.** TR: B29

It's cold. I'm wearing a coat.

It's hot. He's wearing shorts.

5 **Listen.** Stick and say. TR: B30

| 1 | 2 | 3 | 4 |
| 5 | 6 | 7 | 8 |

6 **Listen and point.** Say. TR: B31

a rectangle   a triangle

7 **Listen and colour.** TR: B32

I.

2.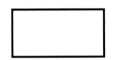

3.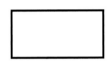

4.

5.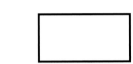

6.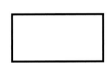

8 **Listen.** Count and say. TR: B33

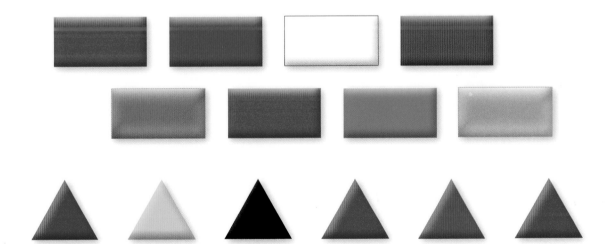

9 **Cut out the cards on page 93.** Listen.
Put the cards in order. Say. TR: B34

10 **Listen and say.** TR: B35

11 **Listen.** Which words have the sound? Tick. ✔ TR: B36

sound	word I	word 2	word 3
I			
2			
3			

12 **Listen and chant.** TR: B37

I want shoes and a T-shirt.

My sister wants a dress.

Let's go shopping.

Grandma, please say yes!

Clean Clothes

14 **Do you like the story?** Circle.

Animals

African lion mother with cub,
Serengeti National Park, Tanzania

eat

run

walk

drink

a giraffe

a monkey

a zebra

a hippo

a lion

a crocodile

3 **Listen and (circle) yes or no.** TR: B41

1.  yes no

2.  yes no

3.  yes no

4.  yes no

5.  yes no

6.  yes no

7.  yes no

8. yes no

4 **Listen and say.** TR: B42

Is the lion eating?

No, it isn't. It's drinking.

5 **Listen.** Stick and say. TR: B43

1	2	3	4
5	6	7	8

6 **Listen and point.** Say. TR: B44

a heart   a star

7 **Listen and colour.** TR: B45

1.   4.

2.   5.

3.   6.

8 **Listen.** Count and say. TR: B46

9 **Cut out the cards on page 95.** Listen.
Put the cards in order. Say. TR: B47

10 Listen and say. TR: B48

11 Listen. Which words have the sound? Tick. ✔ TR: B49

sound	word 1	word 2	word 3
1			
2			
3			

12 Listen and chant. TR: B50

Look, I'm a lion.

I'm walking.

This is fun!

Look, I'm a zebra

standing in

the sun.

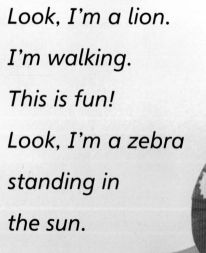

At the Zoo

Look, Teddy. The giraffe's walking.

Look, Teddy. The lion's running.

Look, Teddy. The hippo's drinking.

Oh, no! The monkey's eating my ice cream!

14 **Do you like the story?** Circle.

Review

Start

Finish

Work with a friend. Cut out the spinner on page 95. Spin. Say.

I want a gold crown.

I like bread.

Listen and say. Write. TR: A22

a b c d e f g h i j k l m n o p q r s t u v w x y z

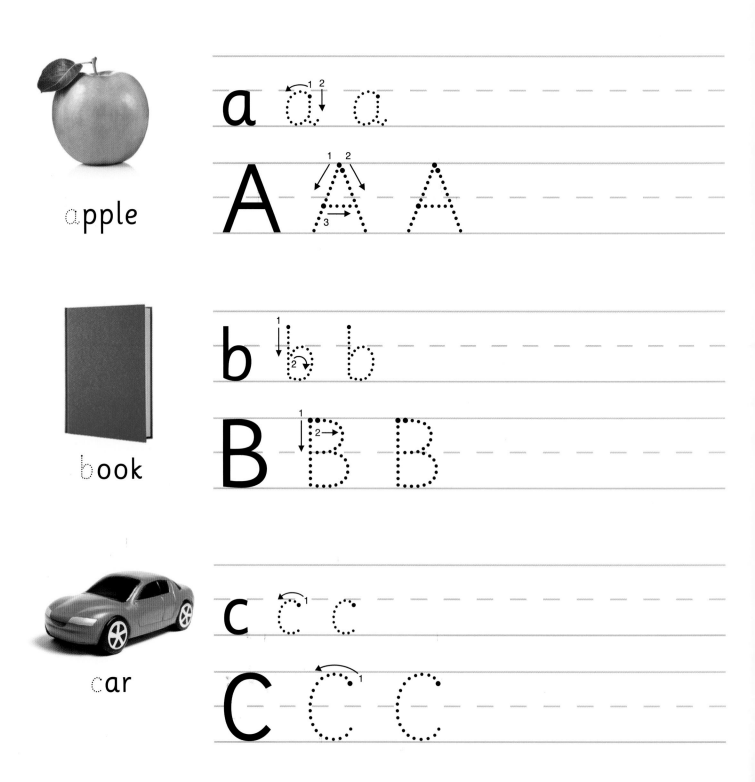

apple

book

car

Listen and say. Write. TR: A36

a b c **d e f** g h i j k l m n o p q r s t u v w x y z

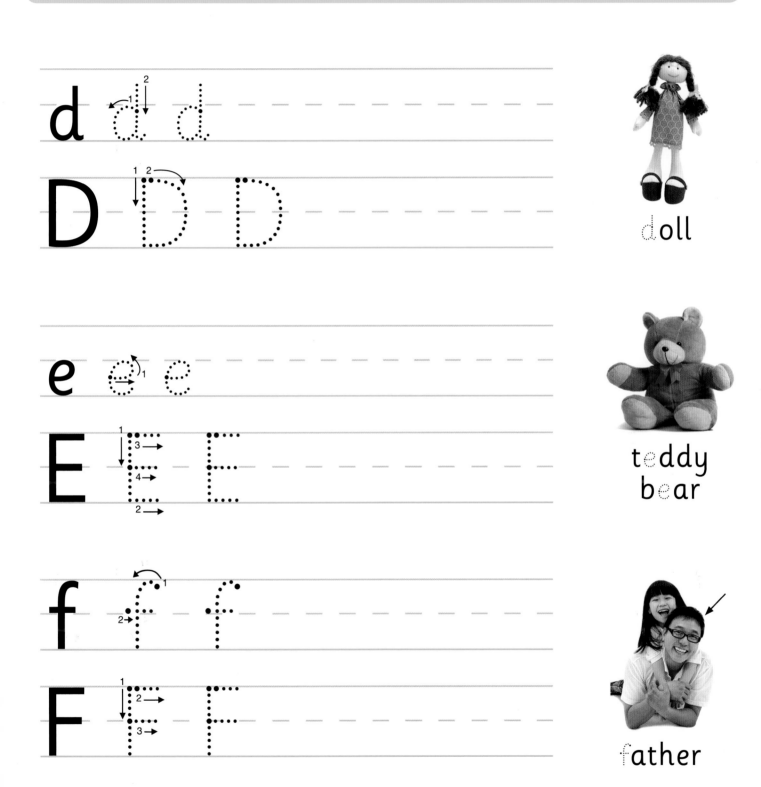

doll

teddy
bear

father

Listen and say. Write. TR: A50

a b c d e f **g h i** j k l m n o p q r s t u v w x y z

grandma

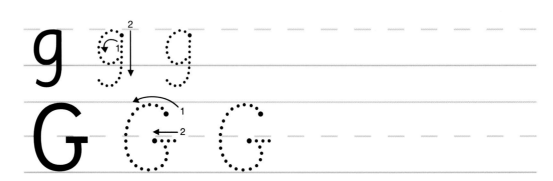

hair

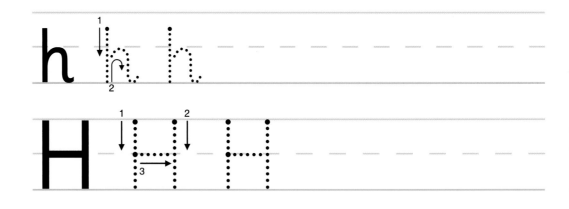

kitchen

Listen and say. Write. TR: A64

a b c d e f g h i **j k l** m n o p q r s t u v w x y z

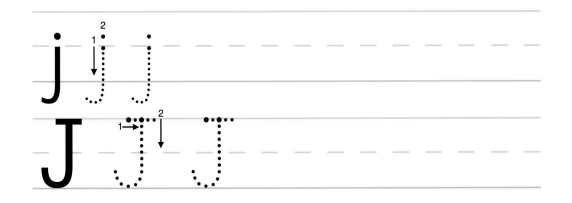

juice

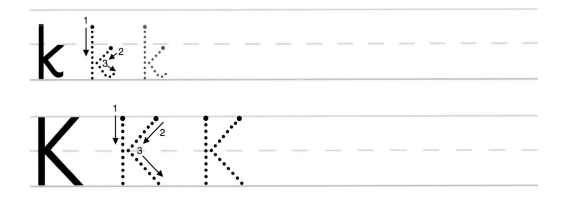

kite

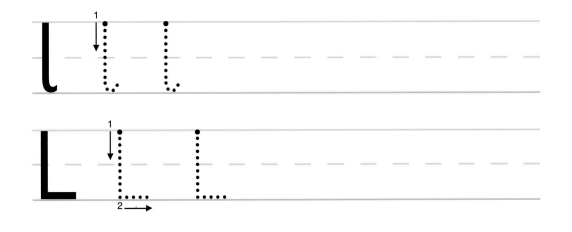

leg

Listen and say. Write. TR: B14

mother

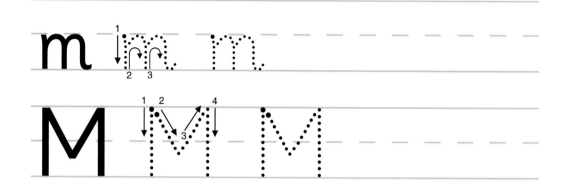

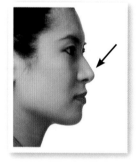

nose

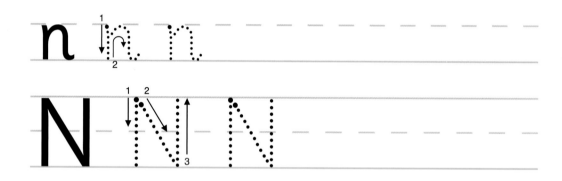

orange

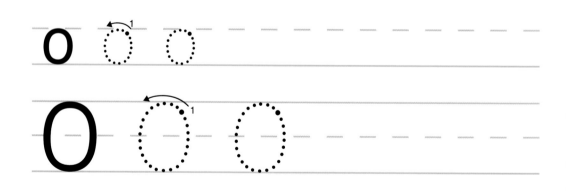

Listen and say. Write. TR: B26

a b c d e f g h i j k l m n o **p q r** s t u v w x y z

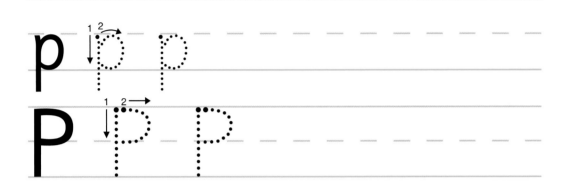

prince

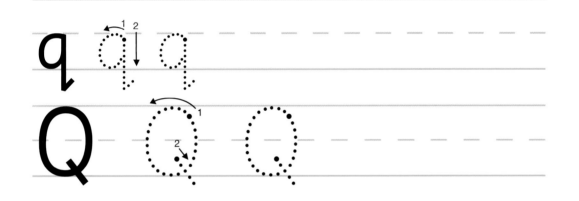

queen

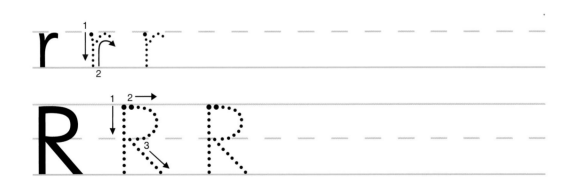

robot

Listen and say. Write. TR: B39

a b c d e f g h i j k l m n o p q r **s t u v** w x y z

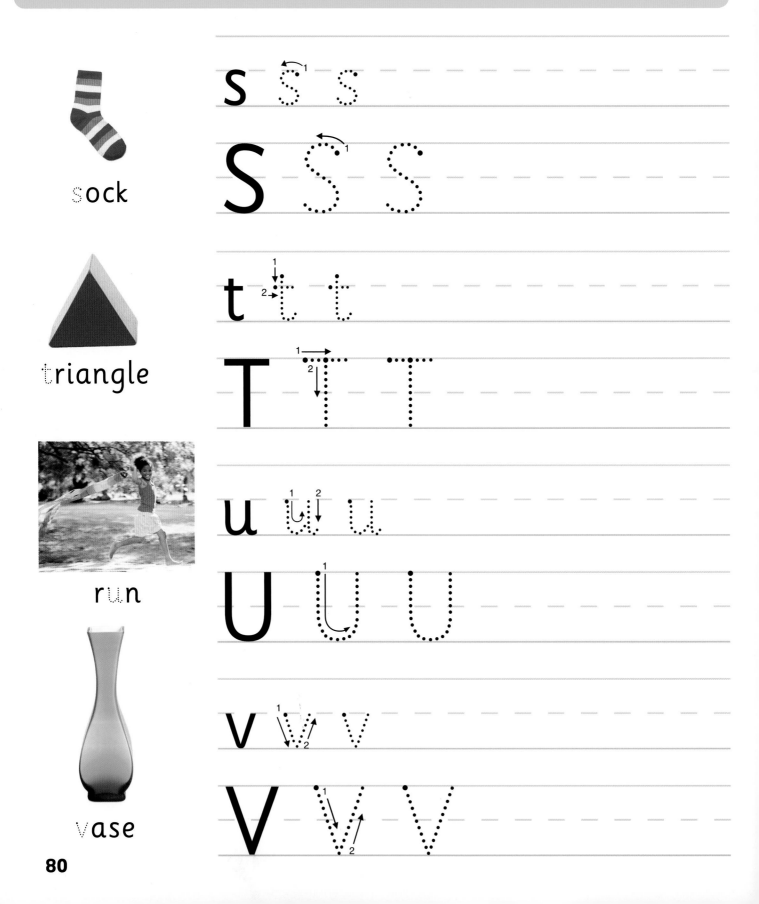

sock

triangle

run

vase

80

Listen and say. Write. Listen to the alphabet chant. TR: B52 and B53

a b c d e f g h i j k l m n o p q r s t u v **w x y z**

water

fox

yellow

zebra

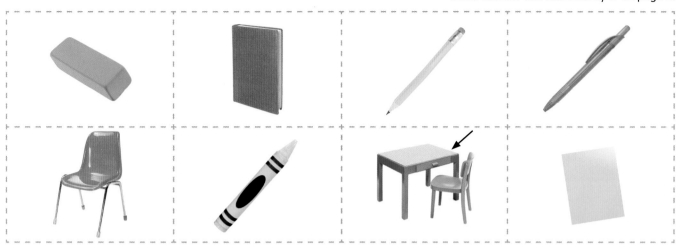

green	yellow
blue	**red**

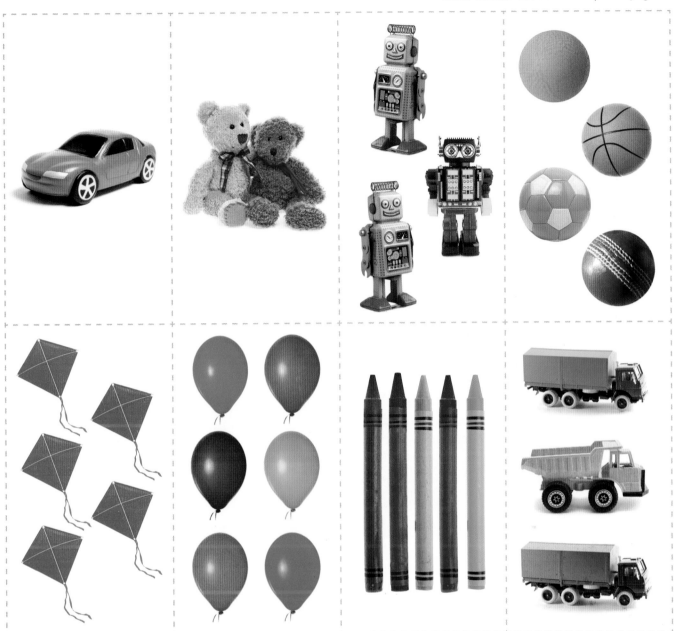

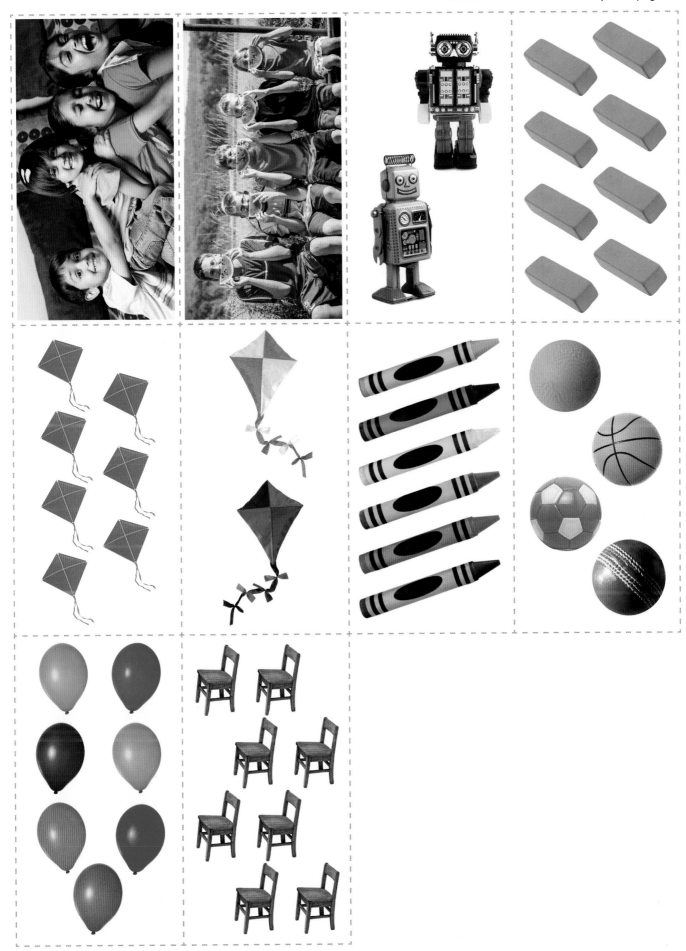

87

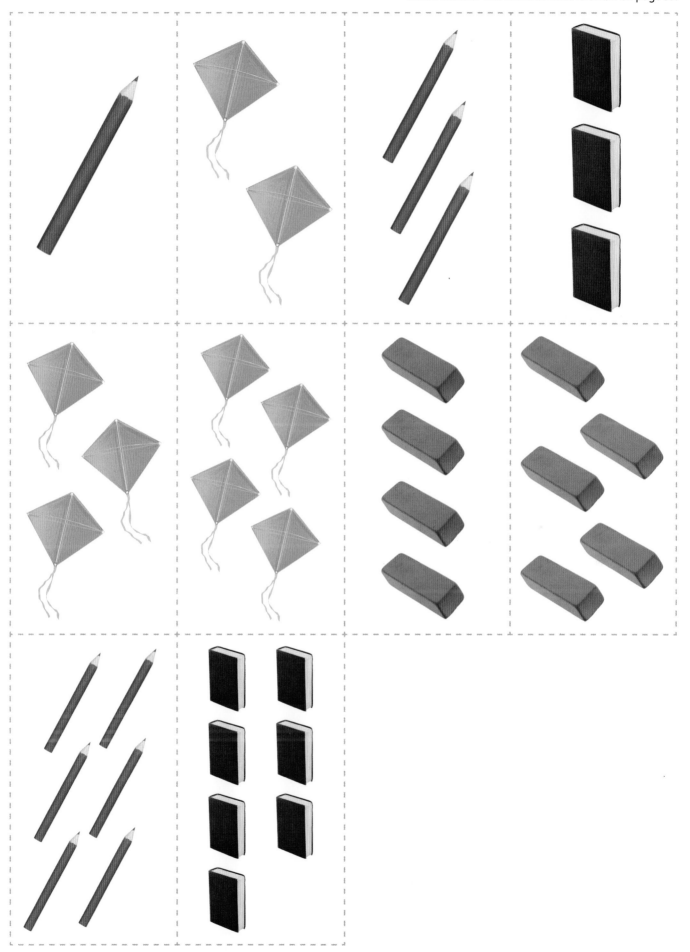

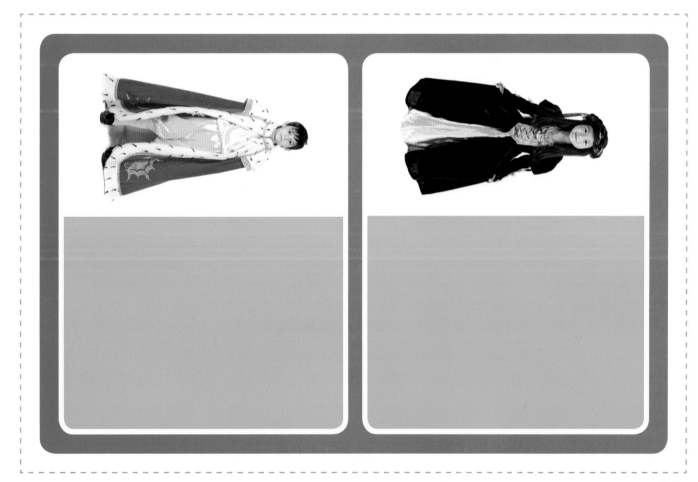

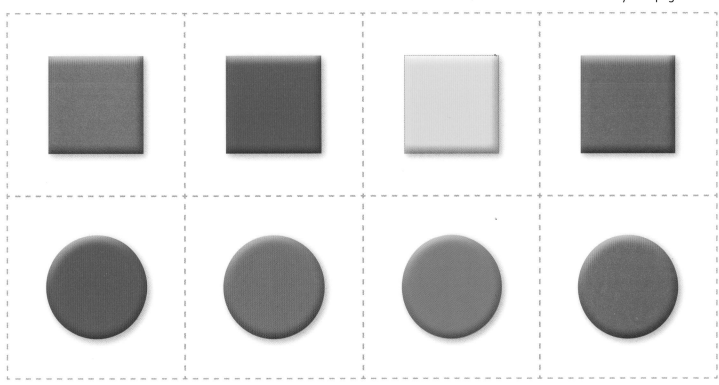

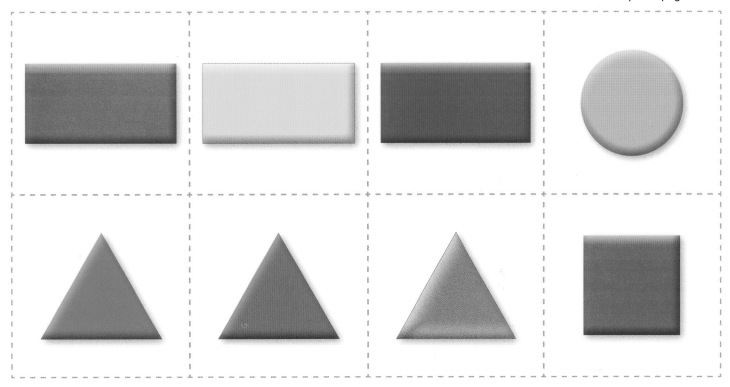

Units 5-8 Review Cutout Use with game on page 73.   **Units I-4 Review Cutout** Use with game on page 39.

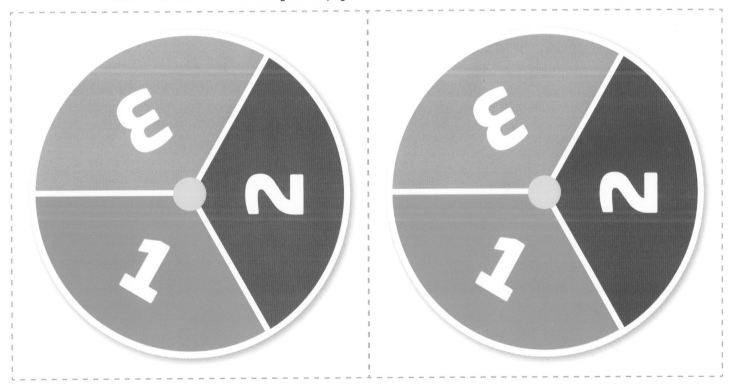